AMERICAN SPELLING

American Spelling

Story in Verse

Andrea Stone

Hedgerow Books

AMHERST, MASSACHUSETTS

Published by Hedgerow Books of *Levellers Press*
Amherst, Massachusetts

Printed in the United States of America

ISBN: 978-1-937146-93-1

For Ken

AMERICAN SPELLING

The Vancouver Sun

May 27, 1974

NORTH VANCOUVER – A province-wide police manhunt continues for a Toronto mother who dropped her child from the 100-meter-high Capilano Suspension Bridge yesterday afternoon, then fled the scene of the accident.

The 2-year-old girl remains in critical condition in British Columbia Children's Hospital, according to a hospital spokesman, who refused to provide further details about the child's injuries or medical condition.

The mother was vacationing with her husband and their two young children when she dropped the child from the famous tourist site at approximately 2 p.m. yesterday, according to a spokesman for the Royal Canadian Mounted Police's North Vancouver office. There is concern the woman may have entered the United States.

1.

Thirty-eight years ago
cold sand
cold snails
sand dollars
seaweed
the sun in the right spot
cut the ropes
cut the questions
released the answer
for a moment—

I dropped my child
from a bridge.

2.

News from home
"Miracle Child Leaves ICU"—The Globe and Mail
"Bridge Girl Stable"—The Toronto Daily Star
"Mayhem Mommy on the Lam"—The Toronto Sun

Globe
Star
Sun

Celestial reportage
of frailty
resilience…

My stranger, my darling
Ma étranger, mon petit chou
I am here to tell you
God help me

Today I halved a peach,
circumnavigated the pit
Its yellow flesh wept

A sliced thumb does the same
cut, pause, bleed

Jesus wept

shortest verse, King James

prelude to a resurrection
foreshadow of another

Lazarus's sisters relieved
un-grieved
hugging in the sun
folds of unmixed fabric mingling
to make shadows
Such is the work of verse and belief

And the bleeding thumb
a kitchen encounter with steel
stainless
painless, at first,
orphaned flap of skin
lonely on a maple wood counter
an accident
your younger sister, an unplanned baby

How can I begin?
The question that haunts

Can I relieve?
Will you believe?
Can you conceive
the impossible
the miracle
that is you?

3.

A seagull beckons
Canadian—shit hawk
Could he circle the globe?
Can I realize my tangled mission?

A micro Magellan in my apartment
on Victoria Street I use paring knives
purchased long after I deserted you
and on my return to this city
now yours

You stop late-afternoons
corner convenience shop after work
Thank You plastic bag dangling, two fingers
black coffee in Dundas Square
then back up to your apartment
unaware I follow your
long auburn hair
I am the known faceless
who watches your back
descend the stair to the subway
later
face surfacing
squinting to sun
the child you were that day…

My voyage of malnutrition, a mostly empty fridge
American oranges in Toronto
a jar of green olives,
old salsa

Look up "land circumnavigation"
You'll find the Northwest Passage

fruitless deadly quests
From exploration comes peach juice, blood, oranges, starvation,
and blankets

Full sphere
the expedition complete...
C'est possible?
C'est vrai?

A cap-pel-la ah
how those syllables involve the whole mouth

The singer started three times
in the midnight ruckus, sacrilege
to the great, dead folk hero
he'd planned to channel
through the channel
channeling
through the fabled passage
now mostly melted
then finally exploded into the mic:
Shut the fuck up back there
I'm trying to sing a song

He made the bar a church

I try to sort it out for you
a combination of sorts should help
sort sorties

The peach lies open, splayed
stone clinging, unturned

fibrous hairs reaching out
lost nerve endings
fleshy edges reddish crying eyes

I will eat this fruit before it rots
Finally follow something through
for you

Some days, she thinks
everything smells
like Windex and mirrors
Meditation born of
walks in wet weather

Snow, high on brown ivy
coats flower boxes when
she recalls how one firm line appeared
She has tried to feel ambivalent
No beginnings of a baby
Has shoved devices in the garbage
with the cardboard packaging
she refuses to recycle
in front of neighbours
The crumpled mess
paper, plastic, and piss
out of her hand
"refuse"
a) to reject
b) garbage
Why is she so at odds with her body?

Popular but sad, the older sister
loathing her dull self
in the vibrant younger's light, waits
She carries neither talismans nor Kleenex
The glowing younger
creamy skin
nearly black eyes
can always spot a phony
The older resents it

The trees wave, skinny russet arms
against an azure curtain
Only little auburn buds
colour of her hair
Brave beginnings
of the promise of leaves
What if she were barren?

5.

The peach smudged knife is sticky
Stainless steel so penetrating
Mingling juices
elements and substances
join, react, counteract
over the smooth surface of
an instrument of creation
and ruin

Myself, my lamp, a peach on a plate

Why deny oneself the pleasure of stealing and denying?
Because I stole from you

I flirt with American spelling for a change
The history
The revolution of letters

Dropped letters—
colour
favour
remind me…of you
child vowel
disavowed
child 'u'

I left one prison for this
I am telling the way out

Twenty minutes later
a Ford sedan rumbles to the curb
like a hungry gut

The older recognizes them
bites into a mint
almost severs her tongue
successive shocks of oral pain
prohibit a smile

The passenger seat throws up the younger
who spits to make her sister look away
She has a belly full of baby
Jerry'll find a place to park

At least one of them is repopulating
The latest loss, their father
Death and reunion, thinks the older,
Her published memoir—Moses couldn't have parted
the sisters more efficiently—
laid their millstone of maternal loss
across the younger's shoulders

He told them she was sick
and had to go away
Gradually they stopped asking

She, the screaming wet ball of baby
the reason their mother skipped out
And now the culprit trudges there
through melting snow
a 3D billboard of fertility

7.

I miss the yellow light
from the kitchen that echoed
in the dining room where
your father stood and smoked
wondering what to do next

He always seemed in the middle
of remembering what was on his mind
I fell for his smoldering beauty
for his head preoccupied with questions
I smiled into the absence of action
and imagined we'd complement

And then we had you
and we did complement
and the whole world envied
and everything shone
and *the angels, not half so happy...*

That's what I remember
There's much will to forgetting

Let me go
Censor that forever, my mind's mouth says

He was a *good* man, friends said
A simple funeral
parish priest
Knights of Columbus
pierogies from their aunt

The older and younger faced each other
at the hospital
the funeral home
the church
the cemetery…

wordless meetings
doing what is done
working to make each tense the past
and then home to forgetting…
and now the late-winter Toronto sidewalk
outside Tim Hortons

The younger is the daughter
no one's mother would have
all thick black heels
beneath thick legs
dark liner
rarely a smile uncharted by sarcasm
yet appealing, forgiveness always an advantage
bestowed on the young
but under the disguise
so pretty
so painfully agonizingly pretty
Christ, why did she try so hard?

In the midst of the older's critique and throbbing tongue
her vacant uterus twirls into a fist—

Crankiness and diminutive mercies

Like homework night
a certain phrase turned her stomach to cement
The younger had said they needed to talk

9.

A secret swells like a broken toe
makes you realize just how important
that little stub is for balance
Quell the yelps and baby it

Your father banned our history from you
"Promise never to come near her—ever"
Words spoken toward the safety glass
of the prison window, stretched out
evaporated like hot breath on a cold day

My hands were shackled
His face a hanging wet towel
only the three-letter word
why

The solicitor's letter arrived yesterday
Your father's death announced
through the mail slot
swiftly with bills and flyers
sealed in a slender manila envelope
First class. Matched his character
Statute of limitations is up now
Poor man
Such a young age
My age

A letter nested within a letter
personal within official
heart within a ribcage
Your father's Parker blue ink
always a fountain pen
trembled out

I went away with our whisper in my pocket
It lived among the lint and spare change

Fat tongue of regret
knotted fearful muscle

His death gives me permission
my mission
to know you

Hope stands in the wings

10.

Different light in different times of day
tells truths you can massage
with a clock, a shadow, the sun
and a dimmer switch
The whole world is sparkling clean
if you tilt your head the right way
Ask a statistician, a politician, a skin condition

A half-year before I let you go
when the north wind would blow into evening
and my *Edmund Fitzgerald* came smashing
fall crept its palsied hand
across the outdoor dining table
on Canadian Thanksgiving
when we planned to take the trip out West
to give me rest

We raised glasses, cuddled kiddies—
you, two years old, your sister, just born—
looked at each other
over bones and streaks of gravy

Your father's smile
a prairie of joy
in me,
a wheat field of fear

Harvest moons and corn, unspoken gratitude
He sang to me—how I wish I could hear him
sing that song again...

Seven months later
the wooden slats on the bridge

bounced with my footfalls
a mute scream
panicked embouchure

his fear behind me
yours below
mine in my throat

11.

Your father ran toward me
baby floundering on his back
eyes frantic
hand over hand
gripping the rail
searching below
how to get down
how to get down

You disappeared
Foliage hiding horror
Nature an accomplice

He turned to me

Frozen legs
muted speech
blurred vision
shortened breath

sweat

instinct

I fled everything
fumbled keys
deliberate ignorance
the certainty of a full tank of gas

Expertise aside
I give you here
a terrible lesson

on failure

fail
lure

hair
frayed
DNA splayed

deadened ends
failure
to maintain
to cut back natural growth
the body's tendency to decay
to fail to curb nature
desire
control

one to another pole

fail
lure

Sin of omission
or commission

Even trying to confess…

what motivated my hands
those phalanges, biceps, triceps
and my mind, pedaling since…

12.

British Columbia's Oakalla Prison
awaiting trial in the Women's Unit:

First doctor
draped in standard-issue white
lab coat sat before her patient

Imagine your brain as the earth
with two poles…

North and South, she meant
But I went to the waves
how gently they slapped at first
the breeze so welcome and welcoming
the onset of something wonderful
I closed my eyes to feel it all
more perfectly
and
smiled wider
ascent, crescendo
exhilarating, battering
winds calling me to wisdom
crow's nest
all seeing
even through wind and rain
knowing just what to do
Yes, this is it!
Blood pounds against the skull
My hands and chest rock with certainty
This voyage will complete

until that moment
before the descent

How the explorers through the passage
must have raced
chased
faced the inevitability
of failure
of fatality

Ice-locked ships
tonnes of steel grind against frost
a heavy-handed halting
How long could they survive?
frozen tissue
frozen bone
scurvy
lead poisoning
botulism
cannibalism

I craned my focus back
but not to the prison doctor
rather to the ships she launched

up there on the bridge
clarity fixed everything
but me

I think that's enough for today.

It's a cold corner on Dundas and Victoria
The younger suggested this Tim Hortons
where someone had been shot out front
Morbid little thing

The older tries to ignore

Back from the lot, Jerry's just in time
to embrace a steaming double double
insinuate his hairy knuckles into neutral space
burden the seesaw in the heavy one's favour

Younger: There's the matter of The House and its
contents.

The matter of The House
House matter
Matters

Family negotiations are a lot like federal politics

Older: Are you up for it?
She glances at her sister's belly.

Soon there will be the pitter
patter pitter patter pitter paterson
little and long so long
in the brief phrases of meadow daisies
fresh from picking in a dewy spring
of buttercups and raspberries
wild as edgewater blues where
she sang through hedges
when she and her sister

would hide and seek
each other in the honey of
clover flowers that stopped them
along the driven way
the older always with the goal
of finding the tangle-haired younger
in an impossible wood bent
over a patch of yellow extremes
seeking something other altogether

14.

Day Five, my unwashed hair
Little sleep
Texas library books draped
the motel room
Books about brains
What had I done?
injury, trauma, damage
on every horizontal surface
open to my
bisyllabic dread
Do not disturb
dangled from the door
a belated request

more than my sick brain

I stopped eating adult food
Stopped bathing

I wouldn't be separated from the books
Somewhere among the diagrams
among the fear and the long words
the punishment
the judgment

If I could just…

Jerry's paler than his teat-twiced coffee
Disappearing into the pallid wall paint,
before her just clothing and hair
An invisible man, the older thinks

Her sister knows her thoughts

The father's things needed sorting, selling
Spring is real estate season
Soon the lawn would come up
Jerry could help
The older continues to watch him disappear
then shifts her gaze

Her sister's belly looks hard, a giant baseball
She hunts for seams she could pick
till it frayed apart

Two apples in an orchard
their father used to say
only variety bound them
that and Sunday dinner
where they stared
from opposite ends
as if at freaks

Older: When are you due?
Younger: June.
Older: I used to have a doll named June
Younger: Jerry's aunt's name is May
The conversation runs out of the room like a motherless duck

Conversation is a golf game—
a reluctant thrill for the retired in colourful pants

What would their dad say now seeing them
landing in bunker after bunker?
Militarized sand traps manicured into a leisure sport
danger imagined everywhere

Older: Have you got the baby's room ready?

She knew the answer
As with most competition
pain is the only way in

Younger: Nearly.

The older's eyebrows
run up the swale of her head

On the green in one

Younger again: Once the Bionic Woman border is up
it'll be done.

Nice putt, two feet from the cup

Knowing *her* she probably found
vintage paper on Queen Street

Younger: I'm buying a crib in the shape of a racecar.
When he's asleep
it'll play the sounds of open-wheel racing.
I hear it's good for developing motor skills.

Just off the rim of the cup

Almost had me, she thinks
Be the big girl

The Lord hates a coward
their father said of the younger's soft shots
sorry breaths, gasps really
till she crawled out of the sand
crisscrossed the green
shoved the ball in her pocket
lit a smoke

There are two people in the world she knows can
hurt her
She is sitting with one

17.

The little ring-tailed daredevil
plummeted through the trees
"Falling is the most common cause
of injury among baby lemurs"
I sobbed
turned off the TV before
learning whether he died
I am a photographer with only one lens

The knife is streaked with peach sweat
now and my fingers stick slightly
apologies for poor penmanship

The older drinks black coffee
No baby present
Hell, go ahead make it wine
There's no one to hurt but me
Never was
May never be

The younger, fidgety,
Fiddles with her stir stick

The older suspects there's more to this
than house prices
furniture auctions
and old clothes
Silent, she presses her with a stare
Jerry dares not move a soft muscle

The younger rummages
pulls history from her purse:
I found these in The House

"Miracle Child Leaves ICU"
"Bridge Girl Stable"
"Mayhem Mommy on the Lam"

Globe
Star
Sun

Silence stretches
sunset on a Great Lake

Outside someone rolls a suitcase over streetcar tracks

A hospital chopper shuttles overhead
The suitcase and the man are gone
The hospital chopper is landing on the roof
A reminder that someone is hurting

19.

I ate only baby food
Gerber glass jars

Strained Peas with Ham
Bananas with Rice
Like a dog
I licked the jars clean

Far away
you lay
an overloaded outlet
connected to wires
and monitors

I continued with the books
imagined your suffering
acceleration/deceleration
the brain rebounds off the skull
forwards and backwards
a malnourished mum rat's moods
I worked my way through the alphabet
aphasia
the loss of language
basal ganglia
uncontrollable movements
cyanosis
blue lips and fingertips…
When I got to zed
I'd have earned my Tomatoes with Rice

How many coffees can I get yuz?
sliced the silence

The Problem Children had one album
the younger could remember
called *Fuck Yuz All*
How she loved her music

Why was the older
their father's favourite
the younger so stubborn
yet so alluring
she, well, the first to arrive
she guessed
timing was all

Now she knows otherwise
his compensation
sympathy
regret

"Miracle Child Survives Fall" – Globe and Mail
"Miracle Child's Mother Missing" – Toronto Daily Star
"Manhunt for Mayhem Mommy" – Toronto Sun

Younger: He kept tons of these.

My God.
I was that girl.
I was that girl.

There. Like eggs laid by a chicken
and stolen by the farmer

One, two, three, four rapidly cooling words
like a cup of coffee on a Toronto winter street

I was that girl.

It would have been better
had it all remained hidden
boxed up
like a dead heart

A woman at the corner table listens in

21.

You saw foam on rocks a few times
as a young child
Can you remember which coast
first waved you over to look
tempted you with its depths
its invisible certainness

The passive one, the leftist one

You were there long ago
and the tides came in
and you dug in your toes
cold sand
cold snails
sand dollars
seaweed
a smile
a photo
the sun in the right spot
little teeth poked through
later that day
that little mouth
gave
a great
holler

What I mean to say
mean
intend
crude
cruel

and on it goes…

and remembering doesn't get any easier
no ease
in this
shifting, smooth pebbles
on a beach declining
toward the water's edge

gravity will always get its way

Cold black coffee gathers a film
in the bottom of a cardboard cup

Older: How long have you known?
Younger: I called you right away.

Right
It was time to leave
She would help
with The House
when she was ready

Winter in this country...
Bronze statue toes point with the compass and
the temperature collapses like an old woman
thudding to her death

and the clock tower winds up

Each second freezes as soon as it's uttered
and the boys and girls wear toques and boots

On each side of the landscape it is wetter
and all people discuss is the weather

In the middle the lost letters
take shape in the air
neighbour candour
each vowel loosened
from the mouth of nonexistence
like a bare white tooth

In winter you looked like a fledgling
in your snowsuit
your little face pushing out
as if from a nesting snag

your miniature hands reached into mittens
always boots were the dreaded moment

Do you still prefer to be barefoot?
Still push your toes
into dirt and sand and mud?
Do you remember anything?

One block
from her apartment
she stops
grey sky above
grey sidewalk below

If my mother still lives
I am not an orphan, she thinks

no answers
only questions
roaring in her head
what of that skull
nearly smashed
she shuts her eyes to it

no recollection
at all of the fall
no connection
to the one who let go

25.

So few understand the moment between cruelty and justice

One summer at our old house,
when you started to crawl
I peered closer at the marble slab before our doorway
A swarming mass caught my eye
Thousands of ants
a colony
converged on the body of a beige moth
daytime
out of its element
Thousands of triply segmented bodies
multiple legs apiece crawled
sprawled
dug in where there was room
not cleaning
but feeding
feasting
colonizing her
ruining her

I started to become
that moth
after I had you

Two hours after the feast
just a shiny marble slab
swarming a memory

all gone

housekeeper to the stars
couldn't have topped the job

Recollection
rec wreck
collection

collect memories if you can
distort with each telling
each untelling

substance
under stance
understanding

Search engines fail
The phone book is useless
The older's is the only apartment
still lit by lamplight

Title of her memoir multiplies in meaning
Absent: One Daughter's Reckoning
I'll say, she thought
More troubling
qualifications in question
abandonment
classic issues:
untrusting, emotionally withdrawn, perfectionist
her need for a baby…

This, though?
How could she locate the invisible?

Third month awaiting trial
I started to eat my hair
pull out one follicle
at a time
relief
one little release
my private courage
concealed in my mouth
swallowed
into my intestinal tract
my stomach

Next
several strands
then clumps
then trouble digesting

Words in the showers
Snickers at cafeteria tables

Then sick
Corner of my cell
Hairball
Not the first
Just the first they found
Infirmary bound

Electric razors sound like hummingbirds
I saw a window box full of flowers
Needle-length beaks darting from
blossom to blossom
emerald feathers shining in morning sun

When I went to bed
I was bald
and I wanted you back

The second time the sisters meet
the sun is working

After emptying The House they lean
back-to-back on the porch

So it's each other or nothing
and the trees keep quiet for once

The younger appreciates collections
The older always puts things right
Buttons, bottle caps, and stamps
for one
Statements, receipts, and addresses
for the other

If the older could box memories
of their mother she would
But there's no rate for shipping such things,
no matter how small the package

The sun sets in Texas pretty much like it does anywhere else
I raised sheep for two years by mistake after my flight

When the rattlesnake bit the lamb
I moved to the city, couldn't take the pain

The lamb's head swelled to
twice its baby size
Within an hour she died in my arms
dusty Pietà in Hill Country

Seeking revenge on rattlers is a bad idea
but anger caring only for itself thinks differently
I needed to save
or destroy something

That day on the way to the bridge
You were becoming me
a baby moth, food for a billion ants
a brain on a marble doorway slab
The sun glinted
And the knowledge sliced through
Cut the ropes
Cut the questions
Released the answer
Euphoria rained down
like health
and then

Jerry is painting the baby's room
The older wonders if he knows what he's doing

and a cloud slouches across the sun like a puffy eyelid

There were boxes to store, The House to sell
finances to sort—all before the baby

Twilight's chill shivers and fingers the feared, bony question:
What happens when the said and done, the done is done, and
can't be undone—
come to fruition?
What happens when real estate papers are signed?

The older and younger split the father's golf clubs
for sentiment only and reluctantly
Solomon's dilemma in irons and woods
But no mother comes forward
The putter is an olive branch bent in a tantrum
the offer of it as crooked as the club but necessary

A sweater is accepted unconsciously
Kindness can be an unconscious trip home

Soon there will be the pitter patter   the pater...

schools sleeping Sundays late
shades of virtue drawn up as examples of good behaviour

and there will be requests for pets   promises
vows to brush   walk   scoop

Younger: Do you think she had some sort of breakdown?

Older: Likely, professionally speaking. She did try to kill me.

Younger: Still, doesn't make us feel any better, does it?

Older: No.

In the boxes sat the knowledge of how but not why

31.

I started eating you
Nail clippings
Mucous
Stray hairs
Flakes of skin
I wanted to house you
embody you
consume you

over
wrought
       whelmed
       done
       processed
       written
       prescribed
       kill

But now age and tablets have rearranged
shuffled the deck on the periodic table

reduced the number of players
changed the dealer

new house rules
new house guests

coping is routine

You made felt dresses for paper dolls
to warm those thin, flat, white girls
with their curlicue yellow hair
Now felt is more verb than noun

past tense
What of tension ever passes?

On the continuum of sad,
where would I put suicide
Smack dab in the middle

Choice is chance in drag

Sad is a three-year-old
a feather in my fantasy
floating down a rainforest
a bowling ball in truth
the misery of physics

I lied to myself nearly every day
Everyone's either trying to remember
or forget something

She helps her sister shimmy into The House
now only taped-up boxes, a rolled up rug
waiting things
The younger edges about them
her belly navigating narrow canals like a blowfish

The older's calves are sore
from putting off orthotics
rubber symbols of having aged

wasteland mnemonics of the
cruel reluctance of rain
of dehydrated muscles
a middle-aged body untended
let go

so much junk, she thinks
and imagines who would rifle
through her things one day

maybe her sister's child
Will they be close?
Will she—
know what to make of her auntie's things?

She opens a box marked "Odds and Ends"
She spends the afternoon across from her sister
with photos of him
and two old dogs—both died of old cars
their dad of old lungs

In the box
a pack of playing cards, a dead flashlight

unopened packet of pink razor blades—
no reason to ask—and a plastic insole

She lines them up on the floor
to see if there was an order to be made

Thing and nothing
Two sides of the same coin

Their mother left two months
after the younger was born

Published last year
an absent parent fills 400 pages...
No matter a father's reticence

As a child, she'd invented mothers:
Mary Poppins, Mr. Mugs, Cher,
Sabrina the Angel—
She figured her mother
like Charlie would call and speak to her
through a box on a desk
give her an assignment she could ace

She never did

She had started searching
stymied attempts
fruitless leads
branches lest leaves
this was a woman
who didn't want
to be found
gave up
and wrote her book

she would be a mother
she would be better

The waterfall records a sigh
and over and over it replays breath
that deludes observers of the living
into thinking it can't be stopped

give us enough time

They finally caught me in Texas
one person in a great big state—read that as you will—

Now, THEREFORE, I, Gerald R. Ford, President of the United
States of America, proclaim and make public the Treaty, as
amended, to the end that it shall be observed and fulfilled with good
faith on and after March 22, 1976, by the United States of America
and by the citizens of the United States of America and all other
persons subject to the jurisdiction thereof.

ARTICLE 2

(1) Persons shall be delivered up according to the provisions of this
Treaty for any of the offenses listed in the Schedule annexed to
this Treaty, which is an integral part of this Treaty, provided these
offenses are punishable by the laws of both Contracting Parties by a
term of imprisonment exceeding one year.

ARTICLE 14

(1) The requested State shall promptly communicate to the
requesting State through the diplomatic channel the decision on the
request for extradition

my lucky year
my offence turned offense

And so, I gave my hands away

And then a grainy
old newspaper
mug shot

dark hair
centre part
slightly layered
puffy eyes
sad
vaguely focused
soft jaw
like hers

Bexar County
San Antonio Police Dept.
8037 – 11-17-76

I remember a sundress I wore in San Antonio
looking at myself in windows on Houston Avenue
Got that job at The Buckhorn Taxidermy museum
—that need for preservation—
I could have been anyone else

Palm trees stretched up from the sidewalk
to a sky blue as a foggy moonlit night in Toronto

I was all white with apple blossoms
pretty as a speckled pup under a red wagon

I tried lipstick as a cure
a perfect shade of rose to match
the blossoms on the dress

Reinvention is far from redress
though the word suggests otherwise

I saw them approach
two men of reproach

gathered me up like a lost letter
told me it would be OK, okay

I surrendered
in front of a 78-point-buck rack
By the time we got to the station
my cheeks were streaked with mascara
It was time

The room swam around me
little schools of yellow-eyed fish
darted past
never close enough to touch
too fast to see
a blur of unity
of conformity
streaks of hue

"Why did you do it?"
A cigarette burned in a corner somewhere
In my mind?
A stroke?
No, that's toast…
In an ashtray
residue the length of a chimney pipe
burning paper
a waste

There was the head asking why again
It wore glasses the size of wrought iron gates
Massive infinity symbols in black ovals
bags of potatoes guarding the entry

Hell gate?
The mouth sounded it out again
and the fish
and the pain
and the wind
and the rain

I couldn't say
In the end
I couldn't say

Younger: My God, the resemblance.

Two bent heads over the image
Silence reigns
The younger reaches a hand
The older squeezes
A kid on a bicycle rides by

Droplets collect and cascade down from
One trumpeter flower blossom to the next
Water falls effortlessly

"You'd had enough of being a mother?"

I closed my eyes and saw you
My answer a wail

Wet leaves smelling like mold
The jumpsuit a hospital gown
felt…

Everything rotting or relinquishing

"They're ready for you"
She held the door handle in its downward position
to conserve energy

The sound of lock unlock lock unlock
a tap dancing tongue on the roof of the mouth
Fred Astaire style
gravity-less, less, no, none
no falling no dropping
the weight of nothing
If only

"Miracle Child's Mother Found"
"Bridge Girl's Mother Arrested in Texas"
"Mayhem Mommy Faces Extradition"

I think the snow has finally run away
after a day of thunder

Snow pretends to say what side it's on
Blotchy grey blemishes work their way through the paint
Splotchy syphilitic sores edge the streets

Snow gets the worst of it:
dousings, severings—autopsied by sharp shovels
but let me tell you…
snow can give as good as it gets

Don't let whiteness blind you

There were days on the inside
when the world was an exoskeleton
I a little heart beating
excess vowels pulsing in a frantic fat heart
intruding like calcium deposits
each word an artery with too many letters
threatening to seal someone up forever

Extradition—nothing extra about it
not in terms of excess
a leaving
another leaving
a vowel returning
a homecoming
a letter 'u' nestled
between an 'o' and an 'r'
Still, a labour

Extra, outside, but on the inside
Extraneous, not strenuous
no matter the beads of sweat

The older starts to say something
(to suggest really)
and then Jerry calls—a disaster
(oil-based paint, closed windows)
They have to leave, check for brain damage

Why did people bother to fix old furniture
the older wonders
helping the younger into the car

Doors of The House are locked
but lights remain hopeful that someone
will come home
put them to bed
Instead they stand sentinel
like scarecrows minus the purpose

Jerry's fine
He's always fine
She would get them sorted
and return

It sits there
as boxes do

A cardboard house of answers...

Alone in the living room
of her childhood, adolescence
more rummaging to do

one lamp
one box
one quest

never so dreading
never so needing
she sifts

"Never allow your hands to go
where your eyes do not go first"
television safety message from her youth
her hands plunge into the darkness of things
What did the television say about her
after it happened?

Faster
more furiously
increasingly curiously
papers.
old passport
his
no sign of hers
dental bills
phone bills

utility bills
and on and on
till she thought
she couldn't go on
and then
an envelope
addressed to her father
her mother's name

return address
from the older's own street
in Toronto
two buildings north
same side of street
her mother's postmark
dated the year the older had moved
to that apartment
no letter inside
he never mentioned

she leans back against
the base of that dusty rose sofa
and cries

42.

When I left Vancouver to go home…
Escarpment followed alongside
the tracks hurtling toward Toronto
an excess of scar tissue
divine massage
might have diminished such build up

Bare trees on the ridge stand up like hairs
protecting the torn tendon beneath its skin

damage
dommage

It's her sister's turn in the game of truth

Older: Do you remember her?

Younger: No.

Older: You were too young.

Older: She was tall, I think…

Her face changes and she blows on the cooling cup

Older again: It's hard to tell if people are tall when
you're two. I'm probably making it up.

They had a mutt named Rudy (after *Rich Man, Poor Man*)
who'd lost his testicles to a snapping turtle
and it was suggested
they put the newly neutered
out of his bleeding misery

But accidental fixing is not grounds for euthanasia
said their dad

Rudy lived to a ripe-old—nearly rotten—
dog's age and never
seemed to miss his balls at all

Older again: You know, he could have told us
she'd died and we never would have questioned it.

Younger: But he didn't.

Older: Maybe he worried she'd come back.

Younger: Maybe he wanted her back.

The older has to go home

44.

I will come
I will come
     and the sky will make way
     and the birds will rejoice
     in the way it should play out

And you, you have come for me
Good quality paper
Fountain pen—just like your father—
To the point
Kind
A request to meet over coffee

One night a rat ran through a restaurant
just as my friend swallowed
his last bite of Chicken Oscar

However, in rare cases a mother [rat] may kill older offspring
(e.g. Babicky and Novakova 1986 found that some
malnourished mothers killed weanling pups).[1]

If knowing is half the battle, what is half a war?

Two halves of the same fruit but not the same halves

At the grocery store I shop for misshapen fruit
the more disfigured the better
so I know they'll not mirror each other
when bisected

---

[1] http://www.ratbehavior.org/infanticide.htm

I want to recognize consciousness after the fact
if in fact it was a fact if in fact it was

You have to pull yourself together
your father said
a tumbling, mimicking mantra
You have to pull yourself together

like a drawstring
I had to tighten
my baggy self

cinch the waist
and squeeze out
shit
blood
regret
guilt
terror

name the seamstress who offers that

Their mother has answered her call
Dread gallops after relief
The older faces herself in the mirror
They will meet

The day of the fall
is an abyss in itself
now filling
like waste
with nightmares
possibly actual vertigo
sixteen floors up
she can't bear to look down
anymore
looks away from the door of the garbage chute
clutches the rail of the elevator
her obsession for a baby
now waning
weaning
What if she tries to kill it
What if she shares her mother's sickness
What will change after today?

46.

Your father once held a sand dollar
up to the sun
convergence of elements on the dog beach

an introduction of sorts, I thought
fire, sand, money

To think about it now
I have to pretend a different ending

You were
wandering around the sand and snails
bracing yourself against the rush
retrievers, beagles, and mutts
you laughed
your pudgy feet in the frigid leftovers
spring at low tide

You hated anything on your feet
except dirt, mud, and grass
always wanted to be
of the earth you were

the baby asleep in the pouch on his back
—I regret how little I knew her—
you, my obsession

diseased clarity
white teeth gleamed
as the sun peered
through the sand dollar

I suppose it cast a shadow somewhere

I am sleepless
every noise appalls me
I am sick with sorrow

47.

You can peel your fingers back
from another's body like an orange rind
you just have to find (or cut) an opening
get it started

I'd become an expert smiler
Sleight of mouth
A trickster

For every scene, every delivered line
outward
a cut line
inward

We'll go on ahead

I overheard a Belgian in America
say my accent was thick
Mine

Maybe it's the maple syrup makes it stick

Where was all the sweet stickiness
that sun-washed day on the bridge?

Mama, up
Mama, up

Each awkward step
You and I one organism crossing
that masterpiece of engineering
your legs dangling at my hips
your arms around my neck

your breath on my ear
Starboard and port of my skull
Waves crashed the hull

hundreds of feet of rainforest
stretched down to a netherworld

greens and browns and humid ecosystems
went about their business
above, the suspension bridge wavered

Your father stayed behind
with the baby on his back
Adjusting straps

I crept along
keeping you
from falling

Like a sparrow in flitting,
like a swallow in flying,
so a curse without cause does not alight

Then the sludge thinned
evaporated
My sorrow lifted with you
my dread
my horror

My euphoria
All together
I believed I would save you

A bald eagle swooped among the conifers
caught me
stopped me

I turned to trace his drawing
a forger of lines in air
the daytime sky unmapped except by him

You can peel your fingers back
from another's body like an orange rind
you just have to find (or cut) an opening
get it started

sublimity can make one cough
it thins the atmosphere
pressure laid bare
unbearable

There was a call from behind
a word uttered
into nothingness
into air
into gone

The eagle ascended
Then dove

48.

Can a narrative be equal parts question and answer?

I have read your book, *Absent*
I was, but I am everywhere in there
The irony of language that calls into being
what is not
and erases
what is

A year ago at the reading…

Oh your skin glowed, those same warm-day cheeks
from your childhood,
your hair the colour of mine twenty years ago
Auburn locks with a slight bottom curl
Your long fingers scratched your name inside
copy after copy

You paused
smiled up at me
and I thought I would die

Brown eyes met
brown eyes
You didn't see your eyes in mine
older
sadder
damper

I…
I almost broke my vow
I…

Perplexed and kind
you waited
I gave you only silence
True to form
only absence and silence

Then, my name
an anagram you couldn't parse

Never this
Never that

I had kept my promise to stay away
At least mostly
Only one I ever have

I cried in the psychology section watching you
continue to sign books
chat with strangers
There's no analysis here, just chance
and cowardice

Since then I have followed
eavesdropped
stalked

added letters where they were dropped
hated every connotation of 'drop'
taken each one personally

I cut fruit in half to pair, to pare one moment
I fear will summarize me in my entirety

This is what they call getting on with it

49.

A full year passed before the start of my trial
I waited in prison
Rarely ate
Barely slept
Darkness at my side
Suicide watch

My charge: Attempted Murder

Pro bono
For the public good

Slick Vancouver lawyer
took me under his pinstriped wing

Sessions with psychiatrists
till he got the answers
he wanted
we needed

My sole metaphor
a ship
tossed
lost

I would not testify
Not unusual
Let us take care of everything

God, what your father must have thought
Gave me a look I could draw today

I'd been struggling

Ever since the baby, he said
He thought I'd made a turn
How I wanted to thank him

Pale, thin, I sat
Listened to each verbal scrape of my brain matter
Each professional swab of my consciousness
Each calculation of my chemistry
Neurotransmitters
Cortical plasticity
Old theories
New theories

One misty recollection
of the day in question
My flight the only recognition
of potential guilt
My mind at the time
incapable
inculpable

Intent
In the end
Impossible to prove

Six months
Hospitalization
Observation
Isolation
Sedation
Acquitted

I punish myself

50.

Your father never knew
for how many years after
I loved him

The snow in winter still falls the same way

The sorry absence of words
Their breathlessness ruptured in silent hope
What a failure to lie fallow
even in winter
To have left my swallows

You have to pull yourself together

I am better
I am alone

We lost an hour last night

I look for it through the windows
as though it might be bicycling
down below, waving back at me
before crossing the sundrenched street

I should be so lucky
with loss

I will arrive early
so as to watch you approach

Usually I follow

I go now…
To meet at that same coffee shop
on the Toronto street
of newly opening leaves
and hospital helicopters
and the anonymous bustling
present and past
where our recent lives converge
As you have asked
and I have yearned
to tell you all I know

Brown eyes will meet
brown eyes again

Here is my attempt to prepare myself
addressed to you
in my terror of just in case

It will slip into the letterbox
as I exit my building
two north of yours
past the shoe store
the theatre
the square
your enveloped history
to tell you your mystery
as complete
as I can make it

Acknowledgments

Very early selections from this book appear in the Spring/ Summer 2007 final issue of *Lichen Arts & Letters Preview* (Oshawa, Ontario). I would like to thank the journal's founders Lucy Brennan, Rabindranath Maharaj, Gwynn Scheltema, and Ruth E. Walker, as well as coeditors during my editorial tenure: Steven Laird, Ingrid Ruthig, Gwynn Scheltema, and Ruth Walker. I learned much from you during our time together.

I would also like to thank those who kindly and generously read early drafts: George Elliott Clarke, Paul Vermeersch, Ian Gogolek, Dan Blaik, Raji Soni, Keith Bridger, Lesley Grant, Brad Smith, Bill Oram, Russ Rymer, and Michael Thurston. As *American Spelling* was nearing completion, Ellen Doré Watson, Naila Moreira, and Michael Thurston's close attention, sharp questions, and honest critique were more useful than I can express.

I am tremendously grateful for Steve Strimer and Hedgerow Books, and particularly Diana Gordon, whose remarkable tenacity, critical eye, and support for this book over the past two-plus years has helped see it through.

Thanks to Martin, Brenda, and Mike Kerry in Malona, Rhodes, Greece who provided great friendship and sustenance while I was scribbling new sections in recent years across the road and in Haraki. Routinely (except once) losing at Scrabble to you Martin afforded me the necessary breaks that allowed for fresh eyes the next day... Thank you (till our next rematch!).

To my mum and dad, Edith and David Gray, thank you for your conversations about the book over many years. The perseverance of my dad, who has read nearly everything I've ever written, merits special attention. You've both been a tremendous support in immeasurable and innumerable ways. Thank you.

To my partner in everything, Ken Ross, this book is for you. Your painstaking attention, critique, encouragement, and advice at crucial stages all have been more helpful than I can say. It's a great pleasure for me to see this book through with you and our dog, Grimsby (who is an awfully good listener).

About the Author

Andrea Stone is an Assistant Professor of literature at Smith College. She is the author of *Black Well-Being: Health and Selfhood in Antebellum Black Literature*. Born in Toronto and raised in Dunnville, Ontario, she received a B.A. from the University of Western Ontario, a B.Ed., M.A., and PhD from the University of Toronto. She lives in Western Massachusetts.